Unprecedented
Press

The Best Kids Explore Ontario © 2025 by Joshua Best

All rights reserved. No part of this publication may be reproduced, distributed, or transmitted in any form or by any means, including photocopying, recording, or other electronic or mechanical methods, without the prior written permission of the publisher or author, except in the case of brief quotations embodied in critical reviews and certain other noncommercial uses permitted by copyright law. For permission requests, email the publisher or author at addresses below:

Contact the publisher:
Unprecedented Press LLC - 229 W Main Ave, Zeeland, MI 49464
www.unprecedentedpress.com | info@unprecedentedpress.com
instagram: unprecedentedpress

ISBN: 979-8-9867126-3-5

Ingram Printing & Distribution, 2025

First Edition

the BEST KIDS explore

FEATURING: maps, reviews, travel tips, and true tales of family adventures

ONTARIO

An illustrated, story-driven travel guide for kids

CONTENTS

MEET THE KIDS 4

LODGING & TRANSPORT 6

STORIES:

WHAT COMES AROUND 8
in Niagara Falls, ON

PUMPKINS & PEANUTS 18
in Vaughan, ON

UP, UP & AWAY 24
in Toronto, ON

LET YOUR HAIR DOWN 32
in Ottawa, ON

LITTLE DETAILS 38

BEST BITES 39

BEST BETS 40

BUMPS IN THE ROAD 42

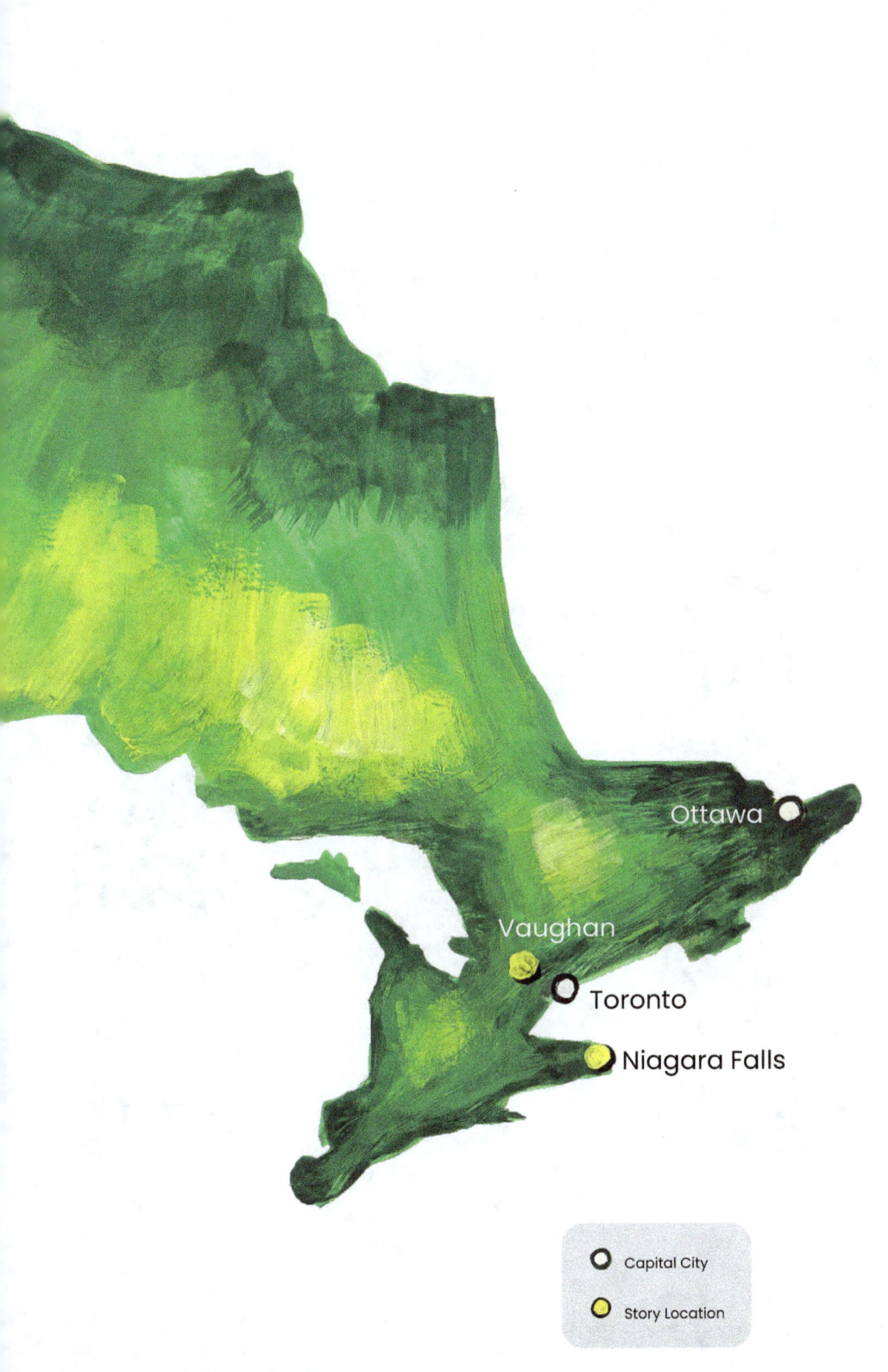

MEET THE KIDS

Exploring is the best. Exploring lets you discover the cool things around you – things you didn't know were there before. That's what makes it so much fun! It's exciting to find out what's around the corner, across the border and beyond the horizon.

The Best kids are explorers. They love finding new places to play and discovering new ways to have fun. The oldest is Frederick – he has orange hair. The middle child is Edith – she has brown hair. The youngest is Hugo – he has yellow hair. The Best kids are half American and half Canadian. They live in Michigan.

In this book, the kids travel to the Canadian province of Ontario. At the time of their expedition, Frederick was nine years old, Edith was seven years old, and Hugo was four years old. This trip occurred between the months of May and June.

LODGING & TRANSPORT

The Best family traveled to Ontario by car – by way of their grey Chevy Traverse to be exact. With snacks packed, movies downloaded to watch and rest stops planned, they traveled east across Michigan. They reached the border in Port Huron and crossed into Canada on the Bluewater Bridge. Their journey picked up in Sarnia, Ontario, and they continued southeast past the city of London and onto their first destination – Niagara Falls.

For lodging, the kids stayed at the Fairfield Inn & Suites in downtown Niagara Falls. Later, they reached the Residence Inn in Vaughan, which was their homebase for visiting Canada's Wonderland and downtown Toronto.

In Ottawa, they stayed at The Groenewegs' house. The Groenewegs are good friends of the Best kids' parents, and they have three kids of their own: Lily, Malachi and Vinny. This was the best lodging of all because it came with good friends, tons of toys, and lots of laughs.

WHAT COMES AROUND

On a pleasant spring day, it was Papa's birthday. This year was a milestone, so the Best kids' extended family were coming together to celebrate. But it wasn't just going to be a party – it was a surprise party. And it wasn't just going to be at home – everyone was meeting up in Niagara Falls.

Like with every road trip, the Best kids packed their bags, and hit the road nice and early. They drove east across the state of Michigan and across the Bluewater Bridge into Ontario. After showing their passports, they were granted entry by the border patrol officers. Everything was going smoothly!

Minutes later, their dad called out, "Something's dinging!"

It was the dashboard alerting him that one of their tires was losing air pressure. All of the Bests looked at each other with worried expressions on their faces. What does that mean? What was going to happen?

"Let's pull over near the mall up ahead and figure out what we should do." said their mom.

So, their dad got off the highway and turned into a nearby strip mall with a sprinkling of big box stores. There, they got out to check the tire, and yes they had in fact, run over a nail. Immediately, the family discussed finding a mechanic shop to fix the tire and continue on their journey, but before they had a chance to look on their phones, Frederick pointed out the window, exclaiming, "Isn't that a tire shop?!"

He was pointing at Canadian Tire, a well known hardware chain in Canada which also sells home goods and auto parts. Apparently, they got a flat tire at the best possible spot, so they pulled up to the store.

With a fresh patch, and some

snacks from inside, the Best kids were back on the road. They were so excited to see their cousins and their grandparents!

As they approached the city of Niagara Falls, they passed through numerous small towns where the speed limit dropped momentarily. In one of those small towns, their dad didn't see the sign, and drove through the village too quickly. The error would have gone unnoticed if it weren't for the police officer, waiting in his patrol car on the outskirts of town. The sound of a siren made everyone nervous, but their mom told them not to worry. The policeman issued their dad a speeding ticket and asked him to be safer next time.

Now with two driving incidents in the rearview mirror,

the Best family was tired of driving. Finally, they arrived in Niagara Falls!

Quickly, the kids hauled their luggage into the elevator at Fairfield Inn and suites. On the third floor, they met their cousins Lucy and Anna, their Uncle Luke, and their Aunt Sarah who were staying there too. Everyone scrambled or to unpack their bags because Nana and Papa would arrive any minute, and Papa didn't know the kids were coming. In fact, he was told he was having a meeting with some colleagues.

With a text alert from Nana, they waited in their rooms while Nana and Papa settled into theirs. Quietly, both families crept across the hall, opened the door to their grandparents' hotel room, and yelled, "Surprise!"

Papa was so happy to see them and celebrate together! After reuniting, they went to check out the falls!

Together, the family walked from their hotel room and along the Niagara River Parkway, a scenic walk up to the waterfalls. On the way up, they stopped for a photo in front of the beautiful, booming water and the orange, setting sun.

At the top of the lookout, there were ponchos offered to visitors because of how much mist came off the falls. The Best kids didn't mind getting a little wet, so they skipped the ponchos. It was amazing to watch the powerful river drop off the side of a cliff with such force! It was thunderous and mesmerizing.

Once they had sufficiently explored the falls and the gift shop, the Best kids and their extended family wandered back down the pathway towards Clifton Hill.

What they didn't realize was that the wind had changed directions, and was now blowing an enormous cloud of mist right onto them! This is what the ponchos were for! This wasn't a few drops; their backs were getting drenched as they ran away in the opposite direction, laughing their heads off!

Clifton Hill is the *Las Vegas-style* strip of Niagara Falls. Everywhere you look, there are flashing lights, carnival, games, and tasty treats. The Best kids settled for a single slice in a triangular box from Pizza Pizza for dinner, and made their way over to the Niagara Sky Wheel.

Standing at over seventeen stories tall, this massive ferris wheel can be quite intimidating. As they got closer and waited in line, the kids started to have second thoughts.

"Are you sure it's safe?" asked Edith.

"How long do we have to stay in there?" asked Hugo.

Once they got to the front of the line and stepped

inside of the pod, they discovered it was heated, played soothing music, had lighting control, and it could seat up to nine people! Unfortunately, all of these bells and whistles didn't make it any less scary.

As the ride began, and the wheel started turning, their pod began to rock back-and-forth, which freaked them out! It took them higher and higher, and eventually they could see the falls. But this time, it was dark and they falls were lit up with colorful lights. Amazing!

After going around three or four times, and wondering if they would ever set their feet on the ground ever again, the ride finally stopped. It was nerve-racking, but it was fun!

The kids gathered their thoughts and talked about the ride over a strawberry funnel cake, which their dad bought nearby.

Niagara Falls had a few surprises, but no matter what happened, they knew as long as they had each other, they would always land on their feet.

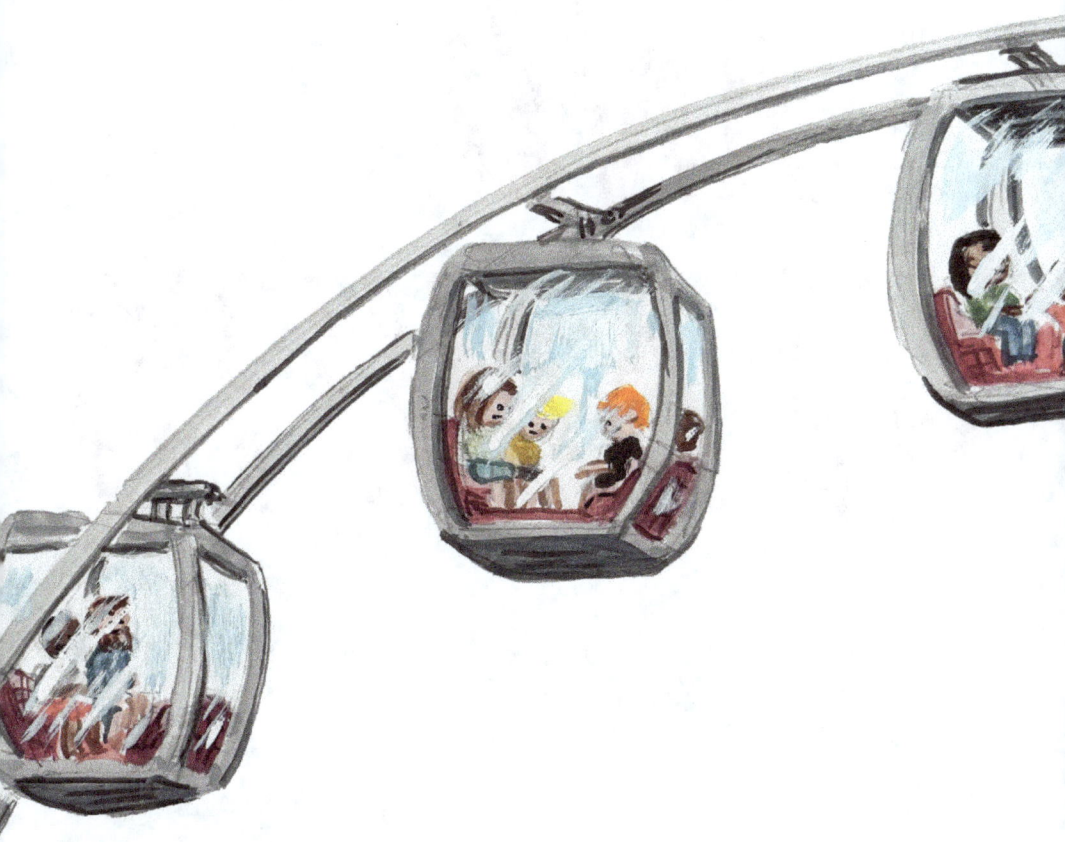

PUMPKINS AND PEANUTS

Sitting in front of a pile of trash, the Best family was coming to terms with the post-Covid, free hotel breakfast. It wasn't as good as it once was, but they didn't care because their hotel was minutes away from Canada's Wonderland – Ontario's preeminent theme park.

They quickly gathered their things, jumped in the car, and were getting excited as they approached the gates – except for the Best kids' mom. She had been here as a teenager and threw up on a ride! She was still willing to come, but she didn't want to go on any rides.

Once inside the park, they noticed the classic roller coaster Dragon's Fyre had a short line. They split up so the big kids could ride it. Frederick and Edith were so

worried about going upside down for the first time that they didn't consider the epic hill at the beginning of the ride. They loved it, and walked off the coaster with wide eyes and hair blown.

Frederick, Edith and dad quickly met back up with Hugo and mom in the Peanuts themed area for kids. Hugo had ridden one small ride, but was gearing up for the big one in this area called Boo Blasters.

"Do you guys want to go on this ghost ride?" Hugo asked the other two.

They agreed enthusiastically and ran to line up. Inside, they were carted through a dark haunted house, and shot creepy characters with green laser guns. Hugo loved it!

The kids continued exploring the park. They flew on Snoopy's airplanes, cruised

in Woodstock's boat, and had their picture taken with Peppermint Patty.

While their mom picked up lunch at a nearby diner, the rest of them stood at the entrance of the Ghoster Coaster – another spooky ride, and Hugo's first roller coaster. With eyes of 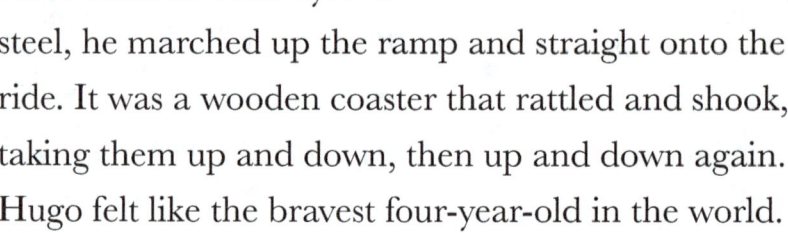 steel, he marched up the ramp and straight onto the ride. It was a wooden coaster that rattled and shook, taking them up and down, then up and down again. Hugo felt like the bravest four-year-old in the world.

In the afternoon, Frederick looked at his mom and asked, "Are you really not going to ride *any* rides? Not even one?"

His mom was quiet for a moment. They could see her trying to overcome her distaste for rides.

"Okay! I'll try one." she conceded.

The kids cheered and looked around for a low intensity ride their mom could handle. Beside the bumper cars, they spotted Linus's Pumpkin Patch, a bright orange ride that lifted you up slowly into the air. Perfect for mom!

As the ride began, the kids' dad stayed below and took pictures. As they floated through the air in the orange pumpkins, the kids realized that even grown-ups find it hard to be brave sometimes. They were so proud of their mom!

UP, UP, UP AND AWAY

On the outskirts of the city, the Best kids walked across the street to the subway station. It was not only their first time riding the TTC (Toronto Transit Comission), it was their first time on a subway train!

They bought a Family Day Pass at the kiosk in the station, and entered through the turnstile. Taking the escalator deep underground was thrilling and eerie at the same time. After waiting for only a couple of minutes, they heard a rumbling sound, and they saw a light shining in the distance. It grew larger and larger until a train burst through the dark tunnel, and came to a screeching halt right in front of them. The doors opened wide, and after other people stepped out, they ran in and grabbed the railings. When the door closed, the subway car jolted forward making Frederick, Edith and Hugo lose their balance.

As the Best family wrote the subway train, the kids learned how to accommodate the backward and

forward motions, as well as the sharp turns. By the end of the journey, they were riding the train like surfers on a big wave.

They got off at Union Station, Toronto's central hub. From there, they walked through a skywalk to reach the CN Tower. The Canadian National Tower is one of the largest freestanding structures in the world, and held the record for the tallest at one point. It is the most iconic part of Toronto's skyline and one of the main attractions in the city.

After passing through security, they reached the elevator which skyrocketed them upwards 114 storeys up into

the air. The elevator had windows for them to see how high they were going, which was captivating, but also terrifying! Finally, they reached the main deck. Their first instinct was to find the windows and look out, but as they walked over, they also found windows on the floor!

It's not common to walk on glass, so this was pretty scary! But the kids took turns daring each other and posing for photos on the glass floor.

The CN Tower was a marvel! And the view was unrivaled. There's nothing in the city of Toronto you couldn't see from the lookout. Later, the kids went up to the highest observation deck (another 33 storeys up)

called the Sky Pod, where they could actually feel the tower moving slightly with the motion of the wind.

The next activity in Toronto was meeting up with Uncle Jamo and Uncle Tobiasz who live in the city. They invited them to eat lunch at a Thai restaurant called Salad King. It was well known in the city, had delicious food, and fantastic decor! Frederick came back to the table from the restaurant bathroom and said, "You have to check out the stairwell!"

Before they left the restaurant, they each went down to the bathroom to see an intricate mirror installation, where murals were reflected in amazing ways!

The next stop for the Best kids was Chinatown, but instead of walking there, they waited on the street corner for a streetcar, which is like a bus, but it runs on a track in the road, and it's powered by an electrical connection high above.

"Ding, ding, ding!"

The street car pulled up in front of them, and after scanning their day passes, the kids boarded.

They rode for nine blocks, and the kids' dad said,

"Edith, do you want to pull the cord?"

Once he explained that pulling a small, yellow cord on the wall of a streetcar alerts the driver to let you off, she agreed with excitement. "Yes, please!"

She pulled the cord, and the kids were instantly transported to a place that looked like a different country! The kids loved exploring Chinatown: the shops, the smell of unkown foods, and the unique, affordable trinkets from street vendors.

With Thai food in their bellies, and Chinese culture all around, their uncle suggested, one more cultural experience – bubble tea (or boba tea as some people call it). So, on the way to Uncle Jamo and Uncle Tobiasz's apartment, they stopped at a Taiwanese bubble tea stand and ordered their favorite flavors.

Frederick got passionfruit tea with mandarin bobas,

Edith got lemon tea with brown sugar bobas, and Hugo doubled down on strawberry tea with strawberry bobas.

As they sat on the balcony of their uncles' apartment indulging in this Taiwanese treat, they reflected on their shifting points of view. They noted how riding an underground train and ascending a soaring tower helped them see the world from a new perspective.

LET YOUR HAIR DOWN

The Best kids arrived in Ottawa, Ontario at the end of their trip. It was their last destination, and they had been away for some time. Not only were they missing home, but they were also starting to look a bit shaggy!

The plan was to stay with some friends of their parents called the Groenewegs. Thankfully, they had kids of similar ages: Lily, Malachi and Vinny.

When they first arrived, they had a great dinner together and played in their backyard where they had bikes, trikes, and lightsabers! Meanwhile, the two

dads talked about the journey up to this point, and how much Hugo needed a haircut. Just minutes later they brought the hair clippers outside.

In the midst of a backyard lightsaber battle, Hugo got a five minute haircut.

With a new morning came a new plan. Ottawa is the capital city of Canada, so they went downtown to explore the sights. The first stop was the Peace Tower on Parliament Hill, the centerpiece of Canada's federal government campus. In front of the tower was the Centennial Flame, a fire that hasn't gone out since Canada turned 100 years old in 1967. Both were majestic to look at, but there was a fair amount of walking to reach it, so Edith was geting *hangry*.

From there, the kids and their newfound friends walked down the street a little further to the Château Laurier,

a hotel that looks like a castle. Mrs. Groeneweg, who is originally from England noted that Queen Elizabeth stayed at the Château Laurier when she visited Ottawa. They considered sitting down for a fancy English tea party, but on this day they opted for a more informal choice – BeaverTails.

The two families continued their walk toward Byward Market, a popular destination for shoppers and foodies visiting Ottawa. They had their eyes, hearts and stomachs set on stopping at the famous Canadian snack spot called BeaverTails.

They pulled up with their strollers, gazed upon the

elaborate menu featuring a wide array of sugary delights on fried dough. After some debate, they landed on a cookies n' cream BeaverTail, and a chocolate with peanut butter BeaverTail topped off with Reese's Pieces.

The two families found a place to sit and share the chocolatey, peanut-buttery deliciousness. With more of it on their faces than in their bellies, the kids ran across the plaza to play and climb on six gigantic letters, spelling out the word, "OTTAWA". Although the Best kids were born in the United States, they're also Canadian, and the joy they found in Ottawa with the Groeneweg family made them feel right at home.

LITTLE DETAILS

SUNGLASSES AT KENSINGTON MARKET

The kids loved shopping for tchotchkes in Chinatown and at Kensington Market. One sidewalk sale had thousands of eccentric pairs of sunglasses, which were fun to try on!

OCAD WINDOWS

In between destinations, the Best kids walked to their dads old campus at the Ontario College of Art and Design. It was a building built on stilts above another building! The stilts looked like giant colored pencils, and the kids we able to sit inside of the deep neon-colored windows on the top floor.

STUNT COASTER

When the kids' mom took the younger two to see a friend, Frederick and his dad got to ride the Stunt Coaster at Canada's Wonderland. Based on the movie *The Italian Job*, it was very fast – a real highlight!

BEST BITES

SALAD KING

In downtown Toronto, Uncle Jamo and Uncle Tobiasz took the Best family to a Thai food restuarant near their dad's college. The name made it sound like their speciality was salad, but it wasn't – just spicy, delicious Thai food. A great experience!

BEAVER TAILS

No tourist's trip to Canada is complete without a visit to BeaverTails. If you like Elephant Ears, try this sweet destination!

PIZZA PIZZA

Ubiquitous but not gourmet by any means, Pizza Pizza is a great quick stop for a large, single slice. The kids loved the triangular orange box it was served in.

BEST BETS

NIAGARA FALLS
NIAGARA FALLS, ON

The walk to the Horseshoe Falls was inspiring and the great mist that overtook the kids on the walk back was unexpected.

CANADA'S WONDERLAND
VAUGHAN, ON

This is a great theme park. Busy, yes. But filled with great rides and also well-maintained.

BYWARD MARKET
OTTAWA, ON

A happening place downtown with great restaurants, and good photo opportunities.

CN TOWER
TORONTO, ON

An epic elevator ride rockets you 147 storeys into the air, and the view from the top is unbelievable.

CHINATOWN & KENSINGTON MARKET
TORONTO, ON

This downtown retail area was super authentic and offered unique buys.

BUMPS IN THE ROAD

TTC DETOUR

At one point, while riding the subway, the kids discovered they would have to switch over to a bus for a segment of the ride. They were doing maintenance work on the tracks for a segment of their route. It made for an extra long ride, and a an extra big headache.

SPEEDING TICKET & FLAT TIRE

The Best kids' dad was super embarassed about being pulled over for speeding – not his finest moment. At least the officer was kind about it! And thankfully their vehicle alerted them to the flat tire with enough time for them to fix it at Canadian Tire.

HEIGHT RESTRICTIONS

One challenging detail at Canada's Wonderland were the kids' varying heights. Like most theme parks, ride access is determined by how tall you are. With five years between Frederick and Hugo, they had a height differential of nearly twelve inches, so the Best family often needed to split into groups to go on the rides.

ABOUT THE AUTHOR

The adventures of the Best kids found on these pages were chronicled by none other than their own father. Joshua Best is a writer, and illustrator by night. By day, he is a creative director at a marketing agency. Of all these roles, there is none better than being a dad to Frederick, Edith and Hugo.

FOLLOW ALONG

Why wait until the next book is released when you can find out now where the kids are headed? Follow the kids on Instagram to watch illustration in progress and to see real photos of current trips! Also, check out the website for ways to get in touch, or listen to our podcast on Spotify, Google or Apple Podcasts.

- @thebestkids_explore
- @thebestkids_explore
- thebestkidsexplore.com
- The Best Kids Explore

www.ingramcontent.com/pod-product-compliance
Lightning Source LLC
Chambersburg PA
CBHW071402130526
44581CB00011B/63